How Artists See

Food

Karen Hosack

www.heinemann.co.uk/library

To order:
☎ Phone 44 (0) 1865 888066
🖹 Send a fax to 44 (0) 1865 314091
💻 Visit the Heinemann Bookshop at www.heinemann.co.uk/library to browse our catalogue and order online.

First published in Great Britain by Heinemann Library, Halley Court, Jordan Hill, Oxford OX2 8EJ, part of Harcourt Education.
Heinemann is a registered trademark of Harcourt Education Ltd.

Editorial: Andrew Farrow and Dan Nunn
Design: Ron Kamen and Celia Floyd
Illustrations: Jo Brooker
Picture Research: Mica Brancic and Charlotte Lippman
Production: Viv Hichens

Originated by Dot Gradations Ltd
Printed and bound in China by South China Printing Company

The paper used to print this book comes from sustainable resources.

ISBN 0 431 93221 2 (hardback)
08 07 06 05 04
10 9 8 7 6 5 4 3 2 1

ISBN 0 431 93228 X (paperback)
09 08 07 06 05
10 9 8 7 6 5 4 3 2 1

British Library Cataloguing in Publication Data

Hosack, Karen
  Food. – (How artists see)
  1. Food in art – Juvenile literature
  2. Art appreciation – Juvenile literature
  I. Title
  704.9'496413

A full catalogue record for this book is available from the British Library.

Acknowledgements
The publishers would like to thank the following for permission to reproduce photographs:

Alamy p. **28** (Harrison Smith); Amsterdam Rijksmuseum p. **20**; Art Institute of Chicago p. **15**; Bridgeman Art Library pp. **4** (The Andy Warhol Foundation for the Visual Arts, Inc./DACS, London, 2004. Trademarks Licensed by Campbell Soup Company. All Rights Reserved.), **10** (The National Gallery, London), **14** (Collection Lillie P. Bliss, Museum of Modern Art, New York), **24** (© ADAGP, Paris and DACS, London 2004); Cameron Watt p. **18**; Claes Oldenburg & Coosje van Bruggen p. **25**; Corbis pp. **7** (Geoffrey Clements), **22** (John R. Jones/Papilio), **27** (Swim Ink); Edward Weston Archive p. **26**; Mary Evans Picture Library p. **5**; National Gallery, London pp. **12, 13, 19**; Ohara Museum of Art, Japan p. **8** (© Yoshiharu Yasui & JAA, 2004); Scala, Florence pp. **16** (Louvre, Paris, 1990), **21 top** (S. Maria della Grazie, Milan, 2002), **21 bottom** (Rossano Cathedral, Italy, 1990); Sheldon Memorial Art Gallery and Sculpture Garden, University of Nebraska-Lincoln p. **11**; Statens Museum for Kunst, Copenhagen p. **6** (© Succession H Matisse/DACS 2004); Tudor Photography pp. **9 x 3, 17 x 3, 23 x 3, 29**.

Cover photograph (*Gateaux* by Philip Le Bas) reproduced with permission of Portal Gallery, London/Bridgeman Art Library.

Contents

Words printed in bold letters, **like these**,
are explained in the Glossary.

How artists see food

Food is very important in all our lives. We need food to grow and stay healthy. We also use food to celebrate special occasions like birthdays, weddings and festivals.

Artists sometimes show food in their work. Andy Warhol's soup can is very famous. It was an everyday object the artist copied and used in his art.

Campbell's Soup Can by Andy Warhol, 1964

Woodcut from Messiburgo's ***Banchetti compositioni di Vivende***, 1549

This **illustration** was made over 400 years earlier than the soup can on page 4. In the **sixteenth century**, everyday objects in a kitchen would have been cooking pots over a fire or baskets of vegetables, not cans of soup!

Patterns and food

Here, Henri Matisse has painted some onions and jugs placed on a table. He was interested in the basic shapes made by the objects. The lines of the sprouting onions and the decoration on the jugs create a strong overall sense of pattern.

Pink Onions
by Henri
Matisse, 1906

Cubist Still-life with Apple by Roy Lichtenstein, around 1974

This still life by Roy Lichenstein has two different patterns. One pattern looks like wood grain, the other one is dotty. The patterns are separated by thick black lines which make shapes. Some of these are fruit shapes. Can you spot an apple and a lemon?

Good enough to eat!

Grapes by Sotaro Yasui, 1952–53

Artists use **tone** to make objects look real. In this painting Sotaro Yasui has used different shades of the same colour to make the grapes look **three-dimensional**. He has used dark shades to show the shadows, and lighter shades to show the places where the light has caught the surface of the grapes. We call these lighter shades **highlights**.

Did you know?
There is a legend about an ancient Greek artist who painted grapes so beautifully that birds flew in through the window of his studio and started pecking at them!

Paint your own fruit picture using tone

You will need:

- a piece of fruit
- paint (any paint will do, for example watercolours or powder paint)
- a **palette** to mix paint on
- a paintbrush
- thick paper or card to paint on.

Instructions:

1 Choose a piece of fruit as your **subject**, then place it on a surface next to a window.

2 Mix three different shades of the same colour on your palette. Use the medium shade to sketch the main shapes of your fruit.

3 Paint in the tones using the darkest shade for the shadows and the lightest shade for the highlights. You should now have your finished fruit painting!

Textures of food

The objects in this **still life** were chosen for their different **textures**. Artists try to show how objects might feel if we could touch them. For example, the lobster looks hard and shiny. The lemon's flesh seems juicy and its skin waxy. The liquid in the glasses sparkles. Painting different textures is a good way for an artist to show off their skills.

Still Life with the Drinking-Horn of the Saint Sebastian Archers' Guild, Lobster and Glasses by Willem Kalf, around 1653

L is for Lemon Slices by
Robert Heinecken, 1971

This **photogram** allows us to see the beautiful
patterns made by the flesh of a lemon. The image
was made by placing **photograph negatives** on
top of each other.

Food and meaning

In this painting the artist has shown lots of fruits and other food. There are also lots of flowers. In the **eighteenth century**, travellers brought back food and flowers from other countries and tried to grow them at home. A lot of the food shown in this painting would have been very rare and expensive.

Fruit, Flowers and a Fish by Jan van Os, 1772

Did you know?

In the eighteenth century people liked to own paintings of valuable food because it showed that they had rich tastes.

Look at this enlargement of the bottom of the painting on page 12. There is a mouse chewing on a nut! Can you spot any other animals eating their way through the food in this painting? The animals are there to remind us that unless the food is eaten, the food will rot away.

Arranging food

The way that artists place objects in a picture is called **composition**. For this painting, Cézanne arranged the apples, jug and cup on a rumpled tablecloth. The cloth takes the viewer's eye from one object to another. We say that it 'ties' all the objects together in the composition.

Still Life with Apples, Cup and Pitcher by Paul Cézanne, 1890–1900

Still Life with Game Fowl by Juan Sánchez Cotán, around 1600

Juan Sánchez Cotán painted this **still life** in a rectangular box shape. He placed some objects on the floor and hung others from the ceiling. The birds are displayed in a similar way to a butcher's shop window. The melon has been cut into slices so that we can see the inside as well as the outside.

Harvest time

Giuseppe Archimboldo wanted to celebrate **harvest** time by showing food gathered in late summer. He arranged fruit and vegetables in the shape of a cheerful face. Look at the round blushing cheeks and the plump smiling eyes. How many different types of food can you spot?

Summer
by Giuseppe Arcimboldo, around 1573

Make your own 'foodie' collage self-portrait

You will need:

- *old magazines, with pictures of food*
- *scissors*
- *glue*
- *a pencil and some paper.*

Instructions:

1 Find some pictures of food in old magazines, and cut them out. You will use these to make your collage.

2 Using a sheet of paper and a pencil, make a simple outline of your face, including your mouth, nose, eyes, eyebrows and ears.

3 Match up the food pictures with different parts of your face, and glue the pictures in place. You should now have your finished **collage self-portrait**!

pie

cake

chilli

pie

leek

Displaying food

This photograph of food is designed to make our mouths water. Look at how the chocolate glistens and the ice cream is freshly scooped. Food stylists arrange food like this to be photographed for adverts and cookery books. They sometimes put paint or wax on the food to make it look even more delicious. Yuck!

This painting shows a very busy market in the **sixteenth century**. The artist has shown lots of **textures** and colours made by the different fruit and vegetables. Some are round and shiny, like the cherries. Others are flat and rough, like the cabbage leaves. All the food at the market has been freshly picked. People did not have fridges and freezers in those days, so they had to shop for fresh food everyday.

The Four Elements: Earth by Joachim Beuckelaer, around 1570

19

Supper time!

Johannes Vermeer liked to paint everyday people doing everyday things. This Dutch woman is preparing a plain meal of bread and milk. Vermeer has used small dabs of white and yellow oil paint to show how the light through the window shines on the food and the woman's face.

The Milkmaid by Johannes Vermeer, around 1657–58

Frescos are pictures painted straight on to **plaster** walls. This fresco by Leonardo da Vinci tells the story of the Last Supper from the Christian **bible**, where Jesus eats with his followers for the last time. The painting covers one whole wall of a dining room in a monastery.

Last Supper by Leonardo da Vinci, around 1495–97

Spot the difference
This sixth-century picture also shows the Last Supper. It was painted about 900 years before Leonardo da Vinci's fresco. How many differences can you see between them?

Food sculpture

A Buddhist food sculpture, made from butter

At the beginning of their new year, **Buddhists** in Tibet make **sculptures** out of butter. Traditionally they sculpt flowers, temple shapes and figures. These are displayed in shrines and in people's homes. The sculptures soon melt in the warm weather. The melting butter stands for how quickly time passes away.

Make your own food sculptures

You will need:

- *a packet of marzipan*
- *a selection of different-coloured food dyes*
- *a mixing bowl*

Instructions:

1 Break your marzipan into lots of small pieces. Next, use a mixing bowl to mix each piece with a few drops of food dye until the marzipan changes colour. Use as many different food dyes as you can to colour your pieces of marzipan. This way you will have lots of different colours of marzipan to build your sculptures with.

2 When you have finished colouring your pieces of marzipan, roll each piece into a ball. You could also roll the pieces into different shapes – it's up to you!

3 When you have done this, mix the pieces of marzipan together to make your finished sculptures. How many different shapes can you make?

Strange uses of food

This is a very odd picture. The man seems to have an apple stuck on the end of his nose! It is painted by an artist called René Magritte. He belonged to a group of artists who liked putting strange objects together in their work. This group was known as the **Surrealists**.

Did you know?

Surrealist paintings were often **inspired** by dreams.

The Son of Man
by René Magritte, 1964

Dropped Cone by Claes Oldenburg
and Coosje van Bruggen, 2001

This upside-down ice-cream cone is huge. The artists
have placed it on a building in the middle of a busy
city. It looks like the cone has fallen out of the sky.
The ice-cream even melts down the side of the
building! It is not really made out of ice-cream though.
It is a **sculpture** made from painted **fibreglass**.

You are what you eat

Have you ever found a piece of fruit or a vegetable that looks a bit like something else? This pepper looks like the back of a person sitting down. It has been photographed carefully so that the light shines off the 'backbone' and the 'shoulders'.

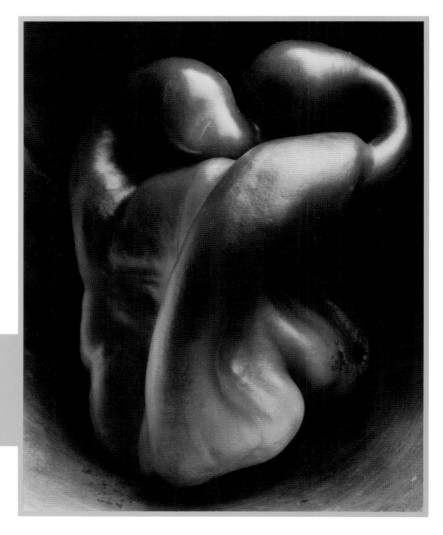

Pepper by Edward Weston, 1930

This is an advertisement. It shows a man made out of sweets, eating more sweets. Does it make you want to buy some? Can you think of any more advertisements that show people made out of food?

Zoom in close

Some artists look at the shapes made by ordinary objects. This fork would normally be used to eat food. It looks more interesting if we just concentrate on its shape, rather than what it is used for. By zooming in close on everyday objects, sometimes we can't even tell what they are at first.

Make your own zoom-in drawing

You will need:

- *some items of food to draw, as well as some other kitchen objects like spoons or a whisk*
- *a pencil*
- *some paper*
- *a magnifying glass.*

Instructions:

1 Choose an object to draw.

2 Make three or four drawings of the same object, each time getting closer and closer. You could use a magnifying glass to help you with this.

3 Show your zoom-in pictures to a friend and see if they can guess what the object is.

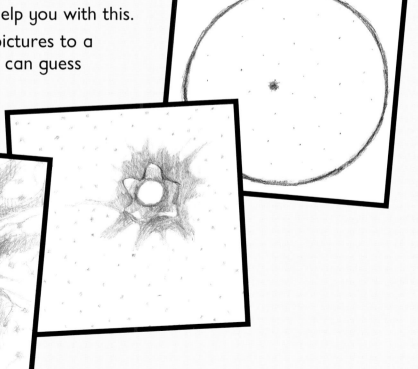

Glossary

bible   the book of the Christian religion

Buddhist   a person who believes in the religious teachings of Buddha

collage   artwork made from materials glued on to a backing

composition   how a painting is put together

eighteenth century   period of 100 years, from 1700 to 1799

fibreglass   a plastic material containing glass fibres

fresco   picture painted on a plaster wall or ceiling

harvest   when farmers gather in their crops

highlight   an area in a painting, showing where light is falling

illustration   a drawing or picture in a book

inspire   encourage someone to do something

palette   tool used by artists to mix paint on

photograph negative   film from a camera that can be used to make photographs

photogram   a picture produced using photographic paper

plaster   a fine white powder that sets hard when it is mixed with water and then left to dry

sculpture   piece of art made from a solid material

self-portrait   an artist's picture of himself or herself

sixteenth century   period of 100 years, from 1500 to 1599

still life   picture of several objects that have been arranged in a particular way

subject   person or thing in a painting or drawing

Surrealists   a twentieth-century art movement

texture   in art, if you give something texture, you make it look how it might feel if you could touch it

three-dimensional   when an object has height, width and depth

tone   light and shade

Finding out more

More books to read

Heinemann Library's *How Artists Use* series:

- *Colour*
- *Line and Tone*
- *Pattern and Texture*
- *Perspective*
- *Shape*

Heinemann Library's *The Life and Work of* series:

- *Auguste Rodin*
- *Barbara Hepworth*
- *Buonarroti Michelangelo*
- *Claude Monet*
- *Edgar Degas*
- *Georges Seurat*
- *Henri Matisse*
- *Henry Moore*
- *Joseph Turner*
- *Leonardo Da Vinci*
- *Mary Cassatt*
- *Paul Cezanne*
- *Paul Gauguin*
- *Paul Klee*
- *Pieter Breugel*
- *Rembrandt van Rijn*
- *Vincent Van Gogh*
- *Wassily Kandinsky*

Websites to visit

www.eurogallery.org – this website lets you search the art collections of important museums and galleries across the whole of Europe.

www.nationalgallery.org.uk – this is the website of the National Gallery in London. All of the works in the collection can be seen online.

Disclaimer
All the Internet addresses (URLs) given in this book were valid at the time of going to press. However, due to the dynamic nature of the Internet, some addresses may have changed, or sites may have changed or ceased to exist since publication. While the author and the Publishers regret any inconvenience this may cause readers, no responsibility for any such changes can be accepted by either the author or the Publishers.

Index